Praise for

"A gripping story about a shameful chapter of our history, when the United States government looked at its own people and saw the enemy."

—Laura Collins-Hughes, *New York Times*

"I wish the current White House, along with young people throughout the nation, could be compelled to attend a performance of *Hold These Truths*....The story of Gordon Hirabayashi reminds us that it is precisely when our bedrock values are hardest to defend that we must stand most firmly behind them."

—Charles McNulty, *Los Angeles Times*

"Hirabayashi's social justice crusade is ultimately galvanizing....The internment policy makes the systemic injustice impossible to ignore, and Hirabayashi becomes a lone citizen fighting government corruption in an increasingly dark saga."

—Nelson Pressley, *Washington Post*

"*Hold These Truths* only makes clear that the hate, ignorance, fear, prejudice and inhumanity of 1942 are still ours in 2018.... If few of us are model citizens the way Hirabayashi was, his story is nonetheless a rallying cry for our own times."

—Lily Janiak, *San Francisco Chronicle*

"...a master class in the personal as political—a play where one man's singular story, so full of heart and heartbreak, can speak to the struggles of an entire nation."

—Julia Hochner, *New York Theatre*

"*Hold These Truths* is what theater should be: instructive, entertaining, thought-provoking, eye-opening."

—Holly Johnson, *The Oregonian*

"Gripping and suspenseful and peppered with both laughter and tears, *Hold These Truths* honors Gordon Hirabayashi's battles, celebrates his ultimate victory, and reminds us of how much still needs to be done, now more than ever. It is far more than a solo performance. It is theater at its most enriching and transcendent."
—Steven Stanley, *StageScene LA*

"Shines an illuminating and searing light on one of the most shameful chapters in US history...*Hold These Truths* is anchored in a historical reality whose rank injustice still boggles the mind more than seven decades later."
—Don Aucoin, *Boston Globe*

"Surprisingly humorous and openhearted...luminous moments of youthful joy arise, too...As *Hold These Truths* reminds us... freedoms are often preserved by individuals willing to stick out their necks for the rest of us."
—Misha Berson, *Seattle Times*

"Mesmerizing and multidimensional...making everything possible is Sakata's lovely, lilting script. She manages to weave a tapestry of experience that is at times funny, at times uplifting, and sometimes, just tremendously sad and shocking."
—Susie Potter, *Triangle Arts And Entertainment*

"I cannot overstate how timely and worth seeing *Hold These Truths* is....an admonition to remember those self-evident truths and practice what they preach even when our elected officials do not.... it is the play's resonant content—about what makes America great and what doesn't—that really gets us where we live right now."
—John Stoltenberg, *DC Metro Theater Arts*

HOLD THESE TRUTHS

HOLD THESE TRUTHS

A solo play by
JEANNE SAKATA

AGELOFF
BOOKS

NEW YORK
2018

In memory of my parents,
Tommy and Lily Sakata.

Acknowledgments

Hold These Truths would never have been written without the encouragement, generosity, and wisdom of many dear friends and treasured colleagues.

Sincere thanks to the following, to whom I will forever be indebted:

Dr. Gordon Hirabayashi, for a remarkable legacy that has left us all with such profound inspiration, for his generosity during our interviews, and for his gracious warmth and hospitality during the time I visited him in Edmonton.

Susan Carnahan and Dr. James Hirabayashi, for reading my initial work and making invaluable suggestions, and for sharing resource materials as well as many endearing memories of Gordon and the Hirabayashi family. Tama Tokuda, Art and Virginia Barnett, Eleanor Ring Davis, Charles Davis, and Dr. Edward Hirabayashi, for sharing their memories, and kind hospitality, as well.

Chay Yew, who believed in the play from the very beginning and in me as a fledgling playwright, and who commissioned me to finish the play, working tirelessly with me till I did.

Len Berkman, Zak Berkman, Morgan Jenness, Douglas Sugano, José Rivera, and Dr. Linda Seger for their wonderful support and guidance in the craft of playwriting. Francis Jue, Marie Masumoto and the Japanese American National Museum, Carla Rickerson and the University of Washington Special Collections Divisions, for their invaluable help with research. Dr. Peter Irons, Kathryn Bannai, and Grant Ujifusa for sharing their legal and legislative expertise regarding the play's events.

Jessica Kubzansky, for joyfully shepherding the play to its world premiere at Los Angeles' East West Players in 2007, and for expertly bringing the script across the finish line; Ryun Yu for his passion in originating the role of Gordon; Tim Dang, Jeff Liu, and the EWP staff, whose enthusiasm and trust made possible our 2007 world premiere, and our co-presenters at the Japanese American National Museum, the UCLA Asian American Studies Center, and the UCLA Department of Asian American Studies, led by Dr. Akemi Kikumura-Yano, Dr. Lane Hirabayashi, and Dr. Don Nakanishi. Marilyn Tokuda, Robert Fromer, Ashley West Leonard, Brendon Patrick Hogan, and John Zalewski for contributing their voiceover work.

Lisa Rothe and Joel de la Fuente, whose generosity and devotion led the play to its 2012 New York off-Broadway premiere, and who contributed weeks of their time for East Coast developmental workshops and readings. Zak Berkman, Ron Russell, Melissa Friedman, Robert Chelimsky, and the Epic Theatre Ensemble, whose dedication and faith made the NYC production possible.

To all my esteemed colleagues who made possible our developmental workshops and readings: Chay Yew and Center Theatre Group's Asian Theatre Workshop; Pier Carlo Talenti, John Glore, and CTG's Mark Taper Forum Writers' Workshop; James Nicola, Linda Chapman, Geoffrey Scott, Toni Amicarella, and the New York Theatre Workshop/Dartmouth College Theater Department; Mia Katigbak and the Consortium of Asian American TheatersArtists/2007 ConFest/Asian American Writers' Workshop; John Clinton Eisner, Daniella Topol, Zak Berkman and the Lark Play Development Center/Epic Theatre Ensemble; Vivienne Benesch and Chautauqua Theater Company; Shannon Mayers and the John Jay College of Criminal Justice; Julie Crosby, Megan Carter, and the Women's Project; Jeanie Hackett and the Antaeus Company; Alice Tuan and Tim Dang and the East West Players Writers Workshop;

To the brilliant directors and actors who took part in our developmental workshops and readings: Jessica Kubzansky, Ryun Yu, Lisa Rothe, Joel de la Fuente, Thom Sesma, James Yaegashi, Mark Schneider, Jake Paque, Clay Storseth, Tessa Thompson, Greg Watanabe, Steve Park, Jason Fong, Kelvin Yu.

Randall Friesen, who designed this publication so beautifully. Ed Salsbury of Impact 24, for his ingenious design of publicity materials, and for the lovely artwork for our book cover. Lia Chang, for her marvelous photos and articles documenting the play's evolution. Barbara

Deutsch, Shawn Tolleson for their inspired coaching.

And finally, Timothy Patterson, my beloved husband, for being by my side every minute of this incredible journey, for never letting me give up, and for his unfailing love, faith and support through forty-one years of marriage.

Foreword

My first introduction to Jeanne Sakata was seeing her on stage in Denise Ueyhara's *Hiro* at East West Players in Los Angeles, where she played the title lead. Luminous, whimsical, and brutally honest, she portrayed an apparition that could fly.

Since then, I've counted myself one of the lucky few who have had the opportunity to closely collaborate with Jeanne both as playwright and director. One of her most memorable performances was her Ovation Award-winning role of a male Chinese opera singer under house arrest during the Cultural Revolution in my play, *Red*. As an actor, Jeanne Sakata is as fearless and ferocious as she is a playwright.

In early 2000, when I was running the Mark Taper Forum's Asian Theatre Workshop, Jeanne approached me with an idea for a play about Gordon Hirabayashi, a University of Washington student who defied the United States government by refusing to register and be illegally interned with tens of thousands of other Japanese American citizens, who were viewed as enemies of the state after the Japanese invasion of Pearl Harbor. Then the 9/11 tragedy happened. I saw history repeating itself when our country quickly turned against Muslim Americans and began illegally incarcerating them. I immediately commissioned Jeanne to write *Dawn's Light: The Journey Of Gordon Hirabayashi*.

Meticulous and always curious, Jeanne would meet with Gordon and ask questions about his time during World War II. She fashioned his anecdotes and responses into a compelling first draft, with which we had a reading at the Taper. Many drafts later, the work was retitled *Hold These Truths*.

That Gordon Hirabayashi does not have a place in our American history books is a cautionary tale to all Americans. What is unsaid, what is unknown, will be repeated. Jeanne Sakata has assumed the role of political activist and educator—in the same fiery spirit of Gordon—by writing this remarkable play, sharing this testimony of resilience, humanity, and citizenship with thousands of Americans in theatres across the country.

Hold These Truths is an essential and powerful work of art, a celebration of an unsung American hero, and an inspiring reminder for us to always resist and challenge great injustices.

Chay Yew
Artistic Director, Victory Gardens Theater

Introduction

When I first heard of Gordon Hirabayashi in the late 1990s, I was enthralled—and shocked. Shocked that I had never heard of his story before.

Born and raised in a thriving Japanese American community in the Bay Area of California, I had studied Japanese-American history as a college student and later became actively involved in the Asian-American community as a theater artist. And yet Gordon Hirabayashi's fascinating story was entirely unknown to me.

Gordon was only a 24-year-old college student during World War II, when he had defied and legally challenged United States government orders to mass incarcerate all people of Japanese ancestry on the West Coast without trial or hearing, including thousands of American citizens—Americans like my own father and aunts and uncles and cousins, who, as children and teenagers, had been forcibly removed from their homes and schools, and penned up behind barbed wire during the war.

My family never spoke about those years, as it was such a traumatic experience. But as I grew up and became fully aware of what had happened to them, I absorbed that pain as well.

So when I finally discovered Gordon's story—so full of heartbreak, but also his irrepressible humor and zest for life—it was a life-changing experience. I knew I had to try to bring his story to the American stage, not just as an act of healing for myself, my family, and my community, but also to inspire and give hope to any American citizen who has been denied equal treatment under the law promised by our Constitution because of factors such as race, gender, sexual orientation, and who must battle constantly to make those promises a living reality.

Gordon's story is a vitally important American one that all of us can draw hope from, and his tenacious quest for freedom echoes those of all who hunger and fight for justice—who "hold these truths" of the Constitution, and refuse to let go.

Jeanne Sakata, Playwright

Hold These Truths

Hold These Truths (under the title *Dawn's Light: The Journey Of Gordon Hirabayashi*) was first commissioned in 2004 by Chay Yew, Director of CTG's Asian Theatre Workshop at the Mark Taper Forum.

Hold These Truths had its world premiere (under the original title of *Dawn's Light: The Journey Of Gordon Hirabayashi*) with the East West Players in November 7 to December 2, 2007, in association with the Japanese American National Museum, the UCLA Asian American Studies Department, and the UCLA Asian American Studies Center. It was directed by Jessica Kubzansky, with set by Maiko Nezu, lights by Jeremy Pivnick, props by Ken Takemoto, sound by John Zalewski, costumes by Soojin Lee. The Stage Manager was Nate Genung.

GORDON HIRABAYASHI   Ryun Yu

Hold These Truths had its New York Off-Broadway premiere in 2012 with the Epic Theatre Ensemble, October 12 to November 18, 2012, directed by Lisa Rothe, with set by Mikiko Suzuki MacAdams, lights by Cat Tate Starmer, sound by Daniel Kluger, costumes by Margaret Weedon. The Stage Manager was Ryan Parow.

GORDON HIRABAYASHI   Joel de la Fuente

Hold These Truths was produced at ACT Theatre in Seattle in July 17-August 16, 2015, directed by Jessica Kubzansky, with set and lights by Ben Zamora, sound by John Zalewski, and costumes by Soojin Lee. The Stage Manager was Michael B. Paul.

GORDON HIRABAYASHI   Ryun Yu

SETTING

The play can be staged in a variety of ways. The set design can be either elaborate and literal, or minimalist and evocative, but in either case, there should be some element of design on stage that suggests Quaker values and principles of simplicity.

For example, a graduated set of platforms can suggest the office, domestic and prison areas, with an open space down center for the outdoors. Antiqued wooden planks or floorboards can suggest a schoolroom, a courtroom, a country fence, or the barracks of the internment camps. Sliding wooden panels or moving flats carrying environmental backdrops, set pieces, and props can serve to suggest different settings. The effects of time and place can be mostly created by light and shadow: a starry sky, a dimly lit jail cell, a country road at dawn. Silhouettes, or images of colored light, can be used to represent specific settings, such as an abstract American flag for the Supreme Court. It may help to have a scrim on stage, on which are projected photos of people, events, and newspaper headlines of the era.

Some of the music in the play should be in the style of old American folk tunes, such as the melodies of Stephen Foster, haunting and evocative, and played on acoustic stringed instruments such as guitar, cello, or fiddle.

For the world premiere of *Dawn's Light*, director Jessica Kubzansky worked with set and projection designer Maiko Nezu and lighting designer Jeremy Pivnick to create striking visual collages and images that reflected Gordon's imagination and subconscious, as well as projections of the words of the Constitution and various government orders. These were projected on two scrims: a larger, stationary one at the rear of the stage for the visual collages, and a smaller, moveable one in front for text. The latter slid along the entire length of the stage to suggest different physical settings: a jail cell, a wall of a building, a fence, a courtroom, an Arizona desert. Ms. Kubzansky also worked with sound designer John Zalewski to create a detailed soundscape for the entire play—crickets, bell chimes, 1940s big band music, war sirens, the slam of a prison door—which sharpened the dramatic essence of every scene. The play was staged on a textured black floor with a raised wooden platform, adorned only with two wooden chairs.

These wonderful contributions belong to the play's original creative team, but I include them here to suggest the possibilities of presenting the story with imaginative simplicity.

CAST

Gordon Hirabayashi

A *Nisei* college professor in his mid-60s, who, while reflecting on his childhood years, "becomes" his younger self—a freshman college student from a devoutly religious Japanese immigrant farming family. His polite, quiet demeanor masks a passionate, idealistic, adventurous spirit. Shy and reserved as a child and teenager, now coming into his own at the University of Washington, Gordon begins to discover his strengths as a student leader and organizer, and also begins to define his spiritual and political identity as a Quaker and a conscientious objector. Painfully aware of the limitations that 1940s America places on him because of his Japanese ancestry, he longs to escape the bigotry, but seems to accept his status as a second-class citizen—that is, until the bombing of Pearl Harbor leads to the mass incarceration of all people of Japanese ancestry on the West Coast, and forces Gordon to take a stand against what he feels is a violation of his constitutional rights as an American citizen.

PLAYWRIGHT'S NOTES

This play is based on a true story, inspired by many hours of interviews I conducted with Gordon Hirabayashi and several of his friends from the 1940s, by numerous letters written by Mr. Hirabayashi during his imprisonment, and by contemporary articles written by and about Mr. Hirabayashi. It is a work blending historical fact with fiction, and certain actual events have been compressed or altered in terms of chronology or content for dramatic purposes. In Act II, Gordon's letters are works of fiction inspired by his actual writings from the Ring Family papers in the University of Washington Special Collections, Accession Number #4241-001. Dramatic license has been taken with the actual historical texts.

The word *Issei* refers to the first generation of Japanese immigrants to the United States, born in Japan. The word *Nisei* refers to the second generation, born, raised, and educated in the United States, and the word *Sansei* refers to the third generation, the children of the *Nisei*.

Special thanks to James Yaegashi for Japanese translations.

Maybe to those who love it's given sight
to pierce the wall of seeming night
and know it pure beyond all imagining...

Maybe to those who love it's given to hear
music too high for the human ear
and clear as hydrogen to go singing...

—Bruce Cockburn, *After The Rain*

Time: early 1980s. In the darkness, we hear a guitar playing a simple melody, in the style of a Stephen Foster song.

A spotlight slowly comes up on Gordon Hirabayashi, a retired Nisei *college professor in his mid-60s. He wears glasses, a tweed jacket and a bowtie. Next to him rests a suitcase.*

He speaks to the audience.

GORDON: "We hold these truths to be self-evident."

Do we, indeed, believe in the existence of "self-evident truth?" Which, by the very rightness of its being, needs no human justification?

And if we say such truths exist, how will they appear to us? In fragments…or in full? Over seconds…or over centuries?

And when they *are* made known to us, how fully will we see them? Will our vision of them be dimmed by the darkness of human corruption?

Our Quaker philosophy of life begins with the faith

of George Fox, who said he saw "an ocean of darkness and death," but also "an infinite ocean of light and love which flowed over the ocean of darkness." And in that moment, Fox said he saw "the infinite love of God."

Rufus Jones, our fellow Quaker, writes, "The ocean of darkness is a fact. The black squares on the great chessboard of the world are as unmistakable as the white squares. The real problem which always faces us is whether the white squares are on a black background, or the black squares on a white.

"The Quaker philosophy of life insists that the black squares are on a white background, and that an infinite ocean of love flows over a finite ocean of darkness.

"This is the basis of Quaker mysticism, and of Quaker optimism, and of the universal spirit of fellowship and sympathy, which belongs to these people who call themselves by the beautiful name of 'Friends.'"

This is what we aspire to.

Aspire. "To seek to attain a particular goal." "To soar to a great height."

And yet, before we are able to soar…

we must often plumb great depths.

For example.

A 65-year-old retired professor of sociology. Who, for over forty years, has sought, struggled—*aspired* to live by such principles, but until this very moment, has never been able to reconcile—

the stigma. The shame. The nagging sleepless voice saying, *No. It didn't happen. I refuse to believe it. The Supreme Court….I will never accept it.*

Yes. If the truth be told…

that voice has never left me.

       Lights slowly change to a soft, dreamlike state.

"Deru kugi wa utareru." Dad first said it to me. "The nail that sticks out is the one that gets hit." It's an old Japanese proverb. To stay out of danger or harm's way, one must conform. One must obey. One must be… inconspicuous.

We'd hear it growing up on the farm during the Great Depression. Hoovervilles. Hobos. Jobless men riding railways. Women and children in breadlines. And Washington state still a western frontier, its settlers hostile to newcomers.

Newcomers, that is, like us.

"Deru kugi wa utareru."

Music: a scratchy Japanese song, played on an Edison phonograph.

Gordon listens quietly, as if hearing his past beckon him. He begins to take off his jacket.

I remember the first time I knew I was Japanese. It was on this lazy Sunday when I was just four or five and my friend Tak was visiting. And Mom served up a picnic lunch: chicken *teriyaki*, *tskuemono* pickles, *onigiri* rice balls...(*savoring this*) banana cream pie. And she put us in the *ofuro*, or outdoor wooden bath. And Tak taught me how to hold my breath, so I shut my eyes and held my nose, and plunged below the surface.

And I opened my eyes underwater and I saw Tak's face. He was blowing bubbles at me and sticking out his tongue. And that watery, blurry image...his nose, mouth, crooked teeth, his brown eyes, his black hair...it was like a mirror. And that's when I first realized I was something....other. Some *ONE* other than what most people around me were. The fact that we were taking a bath outdoors in a wooden tub. The sticky white rice we ate. The prayers in Japanese. It was then it dawned on me: our way of life was "other" in a way I couldn't articulate, but somehow simply...*knew.*

Gordon takes off his bow tie.

Later that day, Mom and I were walking near the railroad. And we saw a dog who'd been hit by a car, and was badly hurt, and whimpering. So I reached out and patted his head, and the dog licked my hand.

"Don't touch that dog."

Mom looked up. She saw a man with a rifle.

"Don't touch that dog."

Mom took my hand.

"Let's go."

"But Mama—he's hurt! He's hurt, Mama, he's hurt."

"*Ima! Ikimasho!*"

And she yanked me onto my feet and pulled me down the road. And by now I was screaming at the man. "He's hurt! He's hurt!"

Sound cue: a rifle shot.

The dog lay still.

"GET OUT OF MY COUNTRY YOU FUCKING JAPS!!!"

That night, when I was falling asleep, my mother came in to tuck me in. And she told me I must never, never, *never* do that again. Speak that way to a white man.

And when the light went out, I heard it again.

"Deru kugi wa utareru."

> *Beat.*

Of course, I didn't always listen to Mom and Dad.

> *Music: Traveling music, guitar and fiddle, in the style of Woody Guthrie.*

> *Gordon exchanges his glasses for another pair, picks up the suitcase and strides forward, transforming into his younger self—a young man in his 20s.*

The University of Washington. Seattle, 1937. I'm a freshman student, newly arrived, when she catches my eye: a pretty blond girl.

> *He nervously, but determinedly, approaches her.*

I ask her if she'd point me in the direction of Eagleson Hall. And then she walks along with me, and says her name is Esther Schmoe, and she says, are you going to the mixer tonight? And I say, geeeee, uh, I don't know,

I really have to unpack tonight and look over the class schedule and anyway I…can't dance.

Esther Schmoe is a *peach*.

"Oh wow, so this is Eagleson Hall? Well hey, Esther, thanks a lot, it was really great to meet you. Yeah, hope to see you around…"

(To himself, watching her go) Hope to see you around… *very* soon.

Esther…Schmoe.

> *Gordon sets his suitcase on the desk and begins to unpack.*

On campus, I've got some pals at the Japanese Students Club. But the rent there is way too steep, so I opt instead for Eagleson Hall, a dorm at the campus YMCA, where there are about a dozen of us, Americans and internationals.

Including my roomie Howie, who becomes my very best buddy. Up to now my best friends have always been other *Nisei*, but Howie's being white is never a problem.

> *Gordon and Howie throw a baseball back and forth.*

"So Gord. *Nisei* is second generation Japanese, born *here*, in America. And *Issei* is the first generation, born over *there* in Japan. Right?

"You're a genius, Howie. Which one am I?"

> *Gordon throws a wild one. Howie dives to catch it.*

"You're someone who can't throw a curve ball for spit."

Howie and I are both dirt poor. We roam around campus like two stray dogs, looking hungry as we can, praying someone will pity us and have us for Sunday supper—roast beef and mashed potatoes, topped with homemade gravy...

Yeah. I miss Mom's cooking. And I even miss Dad's laugh. They're two Japanese *Issei* who are...let's say, unconventional. They belong to the *"Mukyokai,"* a rebel Japanese religious group known as the "Non-Church Movement." Pacifistic. Democratic. No priest. No choir. No *church*. Just four families, "on fire for God," working the land on a commune.

You know how fire produces both light and heat? Well, Dad was our guiding light. Some called him: *"BAKA SHOJIKI!!"* Rough translation: "stupidly honest." When Dad packed crates of lettuce to sell, he never put the best heads on top for the usual grand display. Dad always insisted that…

"Shita no retsu mo ue to onaji jyanakya ikan." "The bottom row has to be just as good as the top!"

And Mom—she was the heat!

Feisty and articulate, she was the family dynamo, who, in another era, would have been a journalist, professor, or politician. She was elected Vice President of our Japanese Association, beating out all the *men*. She wrote poetry and read everything in sight: the *Hokubei Shimbun*, the latest Sears Catalogue—

and her beloved novels. Late at night, by a kerosene lamp, she'd immerse herself in the dungeon scenes of *The Count of Monte Cristo*. Or be swept away to the cotton fields of Tara in *Gone With the Wind*.

"Kono Ashley Wilkes…hmph. No *backbone*, neh. *Kono* Rhett Butler…now that's a real *MAN*."

> *Music: a scratchy 1900s recording of Enrico Caruso singing "Libiamo ne' lieti calici," from the opera* La Traviata.

Mom and Dad, though poor, insisted on some culture. We were the only family around with an Edison phonograph, which played "Finlandia," "La Traviata," and "Jada Jada Jing Jing Jing." And somehow Mom scared up the money for a square grand piano. It was her pride and joy, and strains of Stephen Foster tunes like "My Old Kentucky Home" would waft out the screen door—

> *Music: a piano playing a Stephen Foster tune. Gordon bends over and furiously swings a short hoe, thinning a row of lettuce.*

out to the fields where my brothers and I were hoeing. Thinning. Fertilizing. Hitching the horse to the plow. All of us barely making ends meet. All our work going down the tubes, year after year after year.

I couldn't *wait* to get off that farm. And finally—

I did.

> *Lights change. Gordon gets ready to go to class.*

Now, college is no bed of roses. Those signs I saw when I was a kid—*Japs Keep Out. No Japs Allowed. Japs Not Welcome Here*—they don't disappear. On campus, the Greek row frats declare they're "For White Gentiles Only." And downtown are the usual places where we're turned away. Hotels, restaurants, swimming pools, the orchestra section at the Bijou, where we're banished to the balcony.

But I'm determined. Determined to push on, in spite

of them. And so I take to college life like a fish takes to water.

We hear the bong! bong! bong! of the bell tower chimes.

Okay—not academically. As my folks were always reminding me: "*Gohdon. Anata wa CHONAN dakara.* You are the '*chonan*,' the eldest son." And that meant *pressure*. To succeed, to excel, to set that stellar example. And I was terrified of shaming them in class if I blurted out something stupid. So, as a kid, I'd shrink back in my chair, and pray the teacher didn't call on me.

But outside the classroom—I shone. And now I hit the ground running in the Japanese Students Club, the "Y" Student Christian Movement, seizing any opening I can. As Howie says, "Gord, your *real* major is extracurricular activities."

And soon, those all-night baseball talks turn into political debates. Racial segregation on campus. The rise of fascism in Europe. Whether America should join in fighting it.

As Frank, a Brit, vehemently.

"'Land of the free,' isn't it Gord? So how can you *not* be involved?"

25

"But 'secure the blessings of liberty' doesn't have to mean war. The Constitution also says 'to insure domestic tranquility.' There are times when progress is best made by evolution, not *revolution*."

Not bad for a country hick.

I get elected vice president of the "Y" student council. Get asked to the Sadie Hawkins dance, and *almost* learn to jitterbug. Shop for a church with Howie and find the University Friends.

Friends. I like that. That's what the Quakers call themselves. I'm incredibly drawn to their view that God doesn't reside in any one religion or church, but instead in each man's heart, to be known as each sees fit.

So Howie and I start hanging out there, with Ellie, Helen, Ruthie, Fay. Kenji, Burt. Frank—

and Esther.

> *Delighted, recognizing the girl he met the first day on campus.*

It's Esther Schmoe. With those—terrific eyes. And—

I decide to join the ranks!

> *Lights change. Sound cue: New York City traffic,*

horns honking and blaring.

Gordon picks up his suitcase and walks forward.

Summer of 1940, the end of my junior year. I arrive in
New York for a YMCA leadership training program
called "The Presidents' School." And since the national
student Y is a politically liberal group, we're in seminars
with A. J. Muste and Evan Thomas, advocates of social
action and opposition to war.

And I'm just eating it up.

He puts the suitcase down.

But the question of pacifism isn't an easy one. Fascism
is spreading in Europe—Mussolini in Italy, General
Franco in Spain. Country after country brutally
overthrown by the Germans: Austria, Czechoslavakia.
Poland, Norway. Denmark. And, with England
threatened next, impassioned debates are everywhere—

like at the Union Theological Seminary, where we work
the noontime shift for meals. And then, when we aren't
debating or working—we hit the streets of Manhattan.

Gordon jogs the streets excitedly.

I take the subway everywhere: Chelsea, Harlem,
Greenwich Village. Broadway, Brooklyn, Battery Park.

Everywhere, the blur of the city speeds past my window. Subway doors shut behind my back, not before my face. And in the midst of the city, amid the taxis, subways, trains, and people, people everywhere—

It hits me.

They aren't here.

Gordon stops, staring at a window.

Those…signs in the windows. In the shops, museums or movie theaters. Or even in the coffee shop on 80th with the 15-cent chicken dinners.

I walk into that coffee shop. Just push the door and go inside, and sit down at a table. And no one asks me to leave.

I go to a movie theater. I take my ticket and walk inside. And I sit in the *orchestra* section.

I stand in line at a museum. I pay admission, head inside—

Gordon plays himself and a brusque woman from Queens.

"Hey. You. Come back here."

Here it is. I brace myself.

"That's not enough."

"Excuse me?"

"I said that's not enough."

"Not enough—oh. *Oh.* Not enough money, you mean."

"What the hell do you think I mean?"

"Oh. Right. Let me check. Gee, I don't seem to have it, but—"

"No student discount Fridays. Next!"

"Wait, ma'am, wait—one question please."

"Hey. Wise guy. Step aside. There are all these people behind you."

"If I had enough—I could go in?"

"Enough? Enough *what?*"

"Enough money. The admission price. If I had it, I *could* go in?"

"Jesus Christ. Yeah. You *COULD.* Now *beat* it, buddy.

SCRAM."

>   *Beat.*

I can't go in simply because…I can't *afford* it.

>   *Beat.*

I let that sink in for a minute. Because…because…

I mean, back home in Seattle, I always have to think ahead if I go out with the fellas, or if I take a gal on a date: I can go here, I can't go there, I'll get turned out of the Miramar, better avoid Pacific Street, better take the long way round…

But here…but here…

I spring for lots *more* of those 15-cent chicken dinners. Hit the Metropolitan on Tuesday nights when admission is free. Ride a bus to Harlem to hear a gospel choir, an elevator up to the top of the Empire State Building…

>   *Gordon, reaching the very top, looks down at the*
>   *vast city beneath him.*

and I'm feeling as if some heavy weight has lifted off my chest. Feeling a new surge of endless possibilities. Feeling as if…

I've finally joined the human race.

Lights change. Gordon puts the suitcase away,
back at the University of Washington.

Back in Seattle, I take the plunge. I apply to my draft
board for conscientious objector status. But idealism
won't pay my bills. My trip has left me flat broke.

Enter Woody Woodbury, the director of the campus Y.

"Gordie, you're in luck. The downtown branch of the
YMCA just gave me a call. They need a receptionist at
the front desk from 4:00 to 10:00 pm. And I said I had
just the man."

Good old Woody!

I high-tail it down to the Y, where I pause to read the
bulletin boards, with huge posters of the Y's outreach
in Africa and Asia. And topping it all, a sign: "Young
Men's Christian Association: International World
Brotherhood."

The Y director greets me warmly. He's just returned
from China after four years of field work, and is back in
Seattle to raise more money for the World Brotherhood
program. And since this branch is downtown, he says,
most of their donors will be coming from the Seattle
business community.

Gordon sits in a chair.

"It's a distinguished membership, Gordon, with some prominent citizens, and naturally we have a strategy for how to best approach them. Needless to say, it behooves us to be diplomatic as possible, so that anything that impedes that process, or could possibly be detrimental—"

"Sir, I assure you, I'm well aware of the courtesies that would need to be extended. Now, when would you like me to start?"

The director pauses. Reaches for a glass of water. Takes a sip, clears his throat. Folds his hands on his desk.

"I'm sorry, Gordon. I can't hire you."

Beat. Gordon, taken aback.

"Why not?"

"It's nothing…nothing *personal*, you understand. But as I was just explaining, these donors are absolutely crucial to the funding of our overseas work. And though it is… unfortunate, the possibility may exist that we could… well…offend…you know, potential donors…by hiring… well, by hiring…

"someone like you."

"Someone...like me?"

"Well, times being what they are...you see, when Woody called me, he didn't mention that you were..."

He trails off, and gestures toward Gordon, awkwardly. Gordon sits quietly, searching for a response. Finally, tentatively...

"May I ask a question, sir? I...I'm an *American*. And the campus Y vice-president. So these businessmen whom you say might be...*offended* by my presence. How could they possibly feel that way...and then donate money to 'world brotherhood'?"

The director blinks.

"And excuse me for being so frank...but by refusing to hire me...aren't you...aren't *you*...well, *violating* the spirit of world brotherhood? In your campaign to raise money for world brotherhood?"

The director's face turns red. I can see how badly he feels...how badly he feels for *me*.

But I'm not bailing him out.

Gordon waits. Finally...

"Well. I understand. The situation, that is. Thank you for your time. And I guess this interview's over."

Sound cue: rain.

I trudge back to the dorm under a gray and gloomy sky.

Woody.

Shouting from a distance.

"Hey, Gordie!! So when do you start the job?"

Beat.

Woody feels awful about what happened. And lets me move into his attic, while I look for another job. And while I tend the furnace or sweep the floors or empty out the trash, I tell myself: Look.

There's a *war* going on.

Lights change. Gordon, back on campus, picks up a newspaper.

War. Europe is on fire. The Germans are on the march again in Holland, Belgium, Luxembourg. British forces evacuate in May and June from Dunkirk. Italy declares war on both France and England, and the Germans march into Paris. But now another turn of events:

the alliance at the Axis. Germany, Italy, and Japan
sign a military and economic pact. And now the air is
abuzz with rumors of a Pacific War, and of what the
government is going to do to the Japanese living here.

"Mom. *Shinpai shinaide yo*, don't worry. If they try and
do anything, you know I'll be here to take care of you."

"*Daijobu?* What are you talking about? If they do
anything to the *Issei*, they'll do the same to you *Nisei*."

"Mom, that's impossible. The Constitution protects us,
'cause we're American citizens. Don't worry, okay? Don't
worry."

When the fall quarter of '41 begins, I move back to
Eagleson Hall and catch up with Howie and Esther.
And one quiet December morning, I'm walking to the
Friends meeting house. The sun is shining, the birds
singing…

when Howie comes racing down the stairs.

"Gordie. Japan has bombed Pearl Harbor. The naval
base in Hawaii, Pearl Harbor's been bombed by the
Japanese. The President's declared war. It's all over the
radio. Gordie—you okay?"

It doesn't sound real. It doesn't fit the quiet morning,
the sunshine, the chirping of birds. I hear it, but it won't

register…

America attacked by *Japan*?

No.

No.

> *Gordon rushes to switch on a radio. Sound cue: Voiceovers of radio broadcasts.*

"Fears of an imminent attack by Japan on the West Coast are sweeping through nearly all segments of the public. The entire Pacific Coast from British Columbia to San Diego is preparing for possible raids…"

> *He switches stations.*

"Let's not get rattled. There are thousands of Japanese here who are good Americans. We urge all our listeners that there be no riots, no mob law…"

> *He switches stations again.*

"It would take several Japanese aircraft carriers together with a good-sized fleet of covering war vessels and fuel supply ships, to carry on a sustained campaign against the West Coast…"

Terror grips the West Coast as reports come flooding in. Smashed windows. Death threats. Houses set on fire. *"Fucking Japs! Kill the Japs!"* The FBI knocking on doors. Arresting our fathers, handcuffing them. Young children clinging to mothers as agents ransack our homes. Mothers pleading and sobbing as our fathers are led to jail.

And none of us *Nisei* can escape the shame burning in our faces. Mits, Charlie, Tosh. My buddy Bill Makino. Yuki, Michi, Sumi. Lily, Tommy, Jiro.

Our faces are the faces of the enemy.

> *Gordon, shaken but trying not to show it, grabs a newspaper and reads to his friends:*

"Calm down, *listen*, guys: 'Every effort will be made to protect our alien population from discrimination and abuse...Francis Biddle, U.S. Attorney General.' So we've got the Justice Department's support. And we've got to hope President Roosevelt will stick up for us too."

> *Another friend holds up another paper.*

"Oh yeah? Look at this, Gord."

> *Overlapping voiceovers of more radio announcers as Gordon quickly scans one headline after another.*

"The Japanese in California should be under armed guard to the last man and woman…"

"Herd 'em up, pack'em off and give them the inside room of the badlands. Let 'em be pinched, hurt, hungry, and dead up against it…"

"If they stick around, there'll be Japs hanging from every pine tree…"

"If Seattle ever does get bombed, I think you'll see University of Washington sweaters on the boys doing the bombing…"

"That last one's from CBS Radio, Gord. Edward R. Murrow is blaming Pearl Harbor on *us*!"

Then, in March: an announcement from General John DeWitt, head of the Western Defense Command.

"There will be a curfew. All enemy aliens, or German, Italian and Japanese nationals, will remain inside their homes between 8:00 p.m. and 6:00 a.m., and are forbidden to travel outside of a five-mile radius…

"and this curfew will also apply to 'non-aliens of Japanese ancestry.'"

What the heck…who?

Gordon anxiously reads a notice.

"Non-aliens…Non-aliens of Japanese ancestry."
Someone who *isn't* an alien, someone who was born *here*,
but *is* of Japanese ancestry…

The *Nisei.*

Us.

Me.

It's…..embarrassing. *Offensive.* The President, now
totally consumed with the war effort, is giving the War
Department more authority over our future. And they're
singling us out. German and Italian Americans aren't
subject to the curfew…only us. And rather than the
government admitting that, they're hiding behind this…
this stupid…

> *Gordon picks up his books, then sits down to study.*

But when the curfew is announced, I never think to
question it. And all my dorm mates from the Y become
my volunteer timekeepers.

We're studying at the coffee shop and all of a sudden
José yells out,

"Hey, Gordie. Five to eight."

"Five to eight? Heck."

> *He picks up his books and dashes a lap around the stage.*

And I grab my books, throw on my coat, papers spilling over my arm, and hurry back to Eagleson Hall, waving to other *Nisei* who were scurrying like ants to make it back. And every night is more of the same, till one night in the library...

"Oh, Gordie...five to eiiigghht..."

"Five to eight...*shoot.*"

> *Gordon repeats the lap. Sound cue: rain falling.*

I dash out into the pouring rain. Down the stairs, the courtyard. If I run, I'll just make it. Past the fountain and the flagpole, with the flag drooping in the fog.

The flag.

> *Gordon slows to a stop. He takes a long beat, staring up at the flag.*

And then this question hits me.

Why the hell am I running back?

A swift head turn to look back at the library.

I was born here. Raised here. I'm an American citizen.
And some of my dorm mates...

Increasingly agitated.

I mean, Jose is from the Philippines. And Frank is
British, and Wang Chinese. But *they're* still at the
library. And here *I* am, scrambling like the dickens, just
to get back to the—

"Goooordie!"

I turn around. Some guys from Phi Kappa Phi.

"Hey! Gordie! Eight o'clock! Time to go BEDDIE-
BYYYYYE!"

> *They howl. Sound cue: bell tower chimes. Bong,*
> *bong, bong...*

"Hey Gord. Snap out of it. Criminy, you DEAF?!"

"See you later, fellas."

My friends stare as I turn around and head back to the
library. Across the courtyard, up the stairs, down the

corridor to the left—

I open the door.

"Hey fellas. I'm back."

Eleven heads pop up.

"Gord!"

"Gordie!"

"What the hell are you doing?"

"What are you doing, Howie? Here. Now. What are all of you doing?"

"We're—we're studying."

Gordon sits.

"Yeah. Well I am too."

Lights change. Sound cue: an army official, through a loudspeaker.

"Instructions to all persons of Japanese ancestry...

Posters. Posters. Everywhere. Sides of buildings. Telephone poles. Bulletin boards.

Posters.

"All persons of Japanese ancestry, both alien and non-alien, will be evacuated from the following areas by twelve o'clock noon...

Evacuated...?

"All that portion of King County...beginning at the intersection of Roosevelt Way and East 85th Street.... thence easterly along East 85th Street extended to Lake Washington...

Oh God.

"...thence south along the shoreline of Lake Washington to Yesler Way...thence westerly along Yesler Way to 15th Avenue..."

No. They can't *do* this. We're American citizens...

"...thence northerly to East Madison...thence southwest to 5th Avenue...thence northwest to Westlake Avenue...thence northerly to Virginia Street..."

A long beat. Gordon stands very still.

I stand there for a very long time, letting the rain soak me, letting the shock run through me.

"If anything happens to the *Issei*, they'll do the same to you *Nisei*." That's what Mom had said. That's what a lot of the *Issei* had said.

And I hadn't believed it. I had never believed it.

Despite the firestorm of demands erupting from the Coast. Fueled by the War Department, who insisted we were a security threat, and wanted *all* of us out. Demands for our removal, in the press, on the radio, in the halls of Congress…

"But President Roosevelt would never let it happen." I'd said it over and over. "The Attorney General, the Justice Department, they'd never let it happen. We were born here. We belong to this country. And the Constitution protects us. The Constitution…"

Unable to finish.

The…

humiliation.

Lights change.

The mass exodus begins. Beginning with Bainbridge Island, every district around Seattle rushes to meet its deadline to expel everyone of Japanese blood living within its borders.

We can only take what we can carry. Two suitcases
apiece. And we only have a week to get rid of everything
else we own.

*Gordon rushes to haul furniture from the house
to the yard.*

So we haul it all to the front yard: icebox, stove, washing
machine. Table, sofa, rocking chair. Mom's Edison
phonograph. Her black walnut piano. Dad burns photos,
family treasures, anything suggesting ties to Japan.
Bargain hunters, scavengers, swarm over our belongings.

*Sound cue: Japanese voices over a loudspeaker.
Gordon reads signs:*

**"Japanese evacuee must sell 1937 Pontiac coupe. Four
very good tires, A-1 mechanical condition. Cash
$250."**

**"Japanese evacuee must sell 50-room brick hotel.
Linens, furnishings, steam heat. Living quarters,
garage."**

**"Japanese evacuee must sell fruit market. Complete
stock, fixtures, scales, cash register. Full Price $300."**

The losses are staggering. And through it all, utter
confusion:

"My name is Hazel Woo, and this is my sister Grace. Our mother is Japanese, but our father is Chinese American. Will we have to leave?"

"Colonel Karl Bendetsen? I am Father Lavery of the Maryknoll School. We have an orphanage with children of Japanese ancestry. Some of these children are half-Japanese, others one-fourth or less. Which children should we send?"

"I am determined that if they have one drop of Japanese blood in them, they will go to camp."

At the end of winter quarter in March, I drop out of the university. And since my district is one of the last to go, I sign up with the American Friends Service Committee, a Quaker group helping families move out of their homes. We pack up boxes, arrange for storage, prepare the children to carry their things on the trek to…

to where?

Where are we going? For how *long*?

Nobody has a clue.

Gordon grabs the chair, using it as the driver's seat of a car. Sound cue: car starting up, being driven.

I drive them to the Puyallup fairground assembly center,
where they'll stay till they're shipped to their final
destination. Puyallup, where we'd always go for the
annual county fair. Where we'd pitch pennies, eat hot
dogs, ride the Ferris wheel. But now, when we arrive…

*Gordon stops the car, staring. Puzzled, he slowly
stands.*

Barbed wire.

Miles of it.

Stretched on wooden posts. Snaking across the
fairgrounds. Surrounding the entire…

He realizes.

They're putting us *behind* it.

Beat.

Like pigs. Like cattle. Like…

Gordon runs forward, strains to see inside.

There. Over by the grandstands. They're moving us
into…

Beat.

47

horse stalls.

The stench. I can smell it from where I stand.

> *Lights change. Gordon grabs his suitcase and begins to pack his things.*

May 10th. The day arrives. The notice went up for my district. The day of departure: May 16th. A week. Seven days.

> *He reads a notice.*

"Everyone with one-sixteenth Japanese blood must go."

So I start to pack. Friends drop in to say goodbye, and there's a lot of tears and hugs, so many I have trouble getting it done. I have to rush to finish, and—

> *He drops a book. He picks it up.*

Freshman civics.

"America: Land of the Free."

> *He stares at the book. Slowly, he opens it and reads.*

"We the people of the United States, in order to form a more perfect Union...provide for the common defense, promote the general welfare, secure the blessings of liberty..."

the blessings of liberty...

And the words burn on that textbook page. Each word an eye staring evenly into mine.

He flips to another page.

"No person shall be held to answer for a capital crime, unless on an indictment of a grand jury...nor be deprived of life, liberty, or property, without due process of law..."

Gordon stands transfixed. Then he snaps the book shut.

I phone my friend Art Barnett, a young Quaker attorney, and tell him I've got some questions. I grill him on the Fifth Amendment, and—and—

"Gord? Why are you asking? What the heck are you up to? Gord?"

I hang up the phone.

I get my *Nisei* buddy Bill to come over before I can change my mind. And, after we agonize all night, we shake hands, declaring we'll buck this thing together.

49

But only a few hours later—

Bill.

"Gordie...I gotta talk to you. Gordie...I just can't do it. My parents are getting on, you know, and I'm an only child. So all they have is me, and if something were to happen to them, I would never...I...

"Good luck, Gordie. You've got a lot of guts."

Bill's situation is different from mine. My brothers can look after my folks. They won't be left alone.

But, back in my room at night, I stare at the ceiling, unable to sleep. Heart pounding. Stomach churning.

'Cause now I'm on my own.

And it gets worse from there.

Lights change. Gordon, back at home.

Mom. I break the news to her that night, but the word's already spread like wildfire. She stands there calmly, arms folded. She tells me she agrees with me, praises me for a courageous choice. But these are dangerous times, she says. If I don't go with our family, we may be forever separated. Rumors are flying up the coast that we'll be thrown into jail for years, shipped back to Japan for good, taken to the desert and *shot*.

"Mom. Please. Listen to me. Eddie and Jim aren't kids anymore, they know how to take care of themselves and you and Dad and Dick and Tosh, you don't need me to go with you."

"No. You have a special duty. You're the *chonan*, the eldest son."

Then she lets me have it. Our home is being flooded, she says, flooded with phone calls hourly, from friends, neighbors, relatives, Japanese community leaders.

"You've got to make him change his mind. You've got to make him understand, we *have to* obey the government, we have to prove our loyalty, look at what they're *doing* to us—

Boring into him.

"They're terrified you'll make them suspect too. How can you put them in *danger*? How can you be so *selfish*?"

"Mom—when I was just five years old, and we were at the Seattle Sears. And that guard was staring and staring at you, and you said if they accused you of stealing, you'd protest and sue the police. Then you and Dad lost the farming commune because of the Alien Land Law. And you went to court to fight it."

"*Maketawa*! We lost!"

"Yes. But you *tried!*"

Voices rising, Mitsu pulling out all the stops.

"Do you have any idea what the government could do to you? They might beat you. Torture you. Leave you to starve and die. They could throw you into a dungeon like the Count of Monte Cristo…and I may never see you again. Gohdon, *anata wa chonan desu.* You have a responsibility."

"Yes. I have a responsibility, to live by my own principles."

"Just this once, put principle aside. Gohdon, *onegai!*"

(Shouting) "Mom. *No.* Let me go. I'm going to do this. *I AM.*"

My words hit her like a gunshot.

And then…she crumbles. Sinks to her knees and weeps.

"Mom…"

The lights slowly change.

We part ways.

Gordon, in a daze, slowly walks to the desk. He sinks down into the chair, fighting back the tears.

A sense of time passing, before he can continue. Then he forces himself to take out pen and paper. He sits and stares at the paper. Then, finally, he plunges in.

"May 13, 1942. Over and above any man-made law is the natural law of life, the right of human individuals to life, and to creatively express themselves.

"No man was born with the right to limit that law.

"This order for the mass evacuation of all persons of Japanese descent denies them the right to live. It forces thousands of energetic law-abiding individuals to exist in a miserable psychological and a horrible physical atmosphere. It kills the desire for a higher life. Hope for the future is exterminated. Human personalities are poisoned. Over sixty percent are American citizens, yet they are denied, without due process of law, the civil liberties which are theirs.

"If I were to register and cooperate under these circumstances, I would be giving helpless consent to the denial of practically all of the things which give me incentive to live.

"I consider it my duty to maintain the democratic

standards for which this nation lives.

"Therefore—I must refuse this order for evacuation.

"Signed…Gordon K. Hirabayashi."

> *Beat. Gordon assumes the voice of an FBI official.*

"Mr. Hirabayashi. You are under arrest."

> *Sound cue: jail door slamming. Abrupt light change.*

> *Gordon now behind bars, almost in disbelief. He looks around his cell, trying to orient himself. A sense of time passing.*

> *Finally, he starts a letter.*

"May 16, 1942. King County Jail, Seattle.

"Dear Howie:

"Things are so quiet here on Jefferson Street. The sun out, the air lazy. It is very difficult to realize all that has happened in the last three days, *has* actually happened.

"I'm now being guarded by two splendid privates, Earl Holly of Tennessee and Joseph Jones of Alabama.

"Boy! Have these two got the accent!"

Lights change. The office of Captain Ravisto in the Federal Building.

A Captain Ravisto of the U.S. Army calls me to his office. He offers me a cup of coffee, cream and sugar, a napkin. He briefs me on the success of the "uprooting process." 100 percent cooperation in Northern California. 100 percent cooperation in Southern California. And when we finish our talk, he says he's confident we can *both* achieve the same for Washington state.

"Now, Gordon, here is our proposal. We feel it's a shame your studies have been disrupted by this order. And if you agree to register, we will grant you an early release to continue your education."

"I appreciate the offer, but my answer has to be no. It's a matter of principle."

Beat.

"Yes, of course, I understand. Well, let's *talk* about principle. The principle of *family*. What if we offer early release for your entire family? Shungo and Mitsu, Edward, James, Richard, little Toshiko."

"I'm sorry. I can't do it."

Beat.

"Well, what about *this*? What if the army kicked in a scholarship for your brothers' schooling? We know about Eddie's aspirations to go to Guilford College back east."

"I'm sorry."

(Beat. Sterner.) "Gordon, let me level with you. The number of charges against you could result in a very long prison term."

> *His telephone rings.*

"Captain Ravisto speaking. *(Startled)* Oh...hello, Colonel. It's going very well, sir, and I'm sure we'll be squared away soon...Well, no, he hasn't yet, but our discussion's been very fruitful, and...Yes, Colonel, I tried that. Yes, I tried that too...Yes, I know you are. I'm *very* sorry, sir."

Ravisto hangs up, shaken. I ask if something's wrong. He says that was the Western Defense Command in San Francisco. His superiors at the Presidio, who are obviously paying close attention to the outcome of our talk.

> *Gordon, suddenly realizing. With genuine concern.*

"Oh…hey, Captain, look. I know you're just doing your job, here. And…I hope you're not in any hot water, just because of me."

"Well…let's just say it would help us *all* if you agreed to register."

I look at Ravisto's desk. A photo of his wife and baby girl.

We both sit there, wracking our brains.

"Captain Ravisto—I've got it! Why don't you round up a couple of men to *forcibly* carry me to your car, drive me over to the camp, and dump me off at the entrance? That way you'd get your 100%, and I wouldn't violate my principles."

"You know, that just might *work!* I—wait. No. No. We can't do it. We can't. Military orders strictly state that everyone inside the camps must be signed and registered. If you don't sign, you can't go in. It would be breaking the law."

Beat.

"Breaking…the law?"

> *Lights change. Gordon, back in prison, plays a visitor.*

"Mr. Hirabayashi? State Senator Mary Farquharson. How are you doing in jail? Comfy? Now, how are you intending to fight this order in the courts?"

"Well, Senator, to tell you the truth, I haven't thought much about it. This is my first time...'breaking the law.'"

"Well, I'm part of a citizens' action group here in Seattle. And we want to *do* something. If you don't have plans for a legal battle, would you agree to be our test case?"

A gift out of the blue. I'm going to have some help. I've got no money, no courtroom smarts, no strategy, no game plan. No idea for how on earth I'm going to fight this thing. I just know I have to say no.

But now I jump at the chance to say *yes*. And Mary charges into action.

Executive Order 9066, pushed by the War Department, had given President Roosevelt sweeping powers to expel anyone from the West Coast without trial or hearing. So. Mary's first call?

The executive director of the national ACLU.

"Roger Baldwin here. We've been searching high and low for a test case to challenge these orders. So I hope your Japanese boy will stick. Yes. We'll pay his expenses.

Our national board has just agreed to fully support his case."

Then Art Barnett, my Quaker lawyer friend, scours all of Seattle for a lawyer to represent me.

"Gordie? Got your man. John Geisness, a partner with George Vanderveer, in one of the most prestigious law firms in Seattle. Now Vanderveer is known as a civil liberties *hero*. So this firm's the one for you."

Art had scored. Scored big. And now, my spirits soaring, I declare myself—

"Not guilty."

At my court arraignment, I'm charged with two counts: violation of the curfew, and of the exclusion order. And we ask the judge, if we pay bail, can I be free to walk out of here just like anyone else? But he says no, if the bail is paid, they'd send me to Puyallup.

So I say: No. I'm staying put.

Then another call from Baldwin.

"We've got some—complications. ACLU board members demanding we support the President and not challenge his wartime orders. They've just voted to *reverse* their stand, barring support to *any* legal challenge to Executive Order 9066.

"Which means, we must, regrettably…withdraw support for your case."

The American…*Civil Liberties* Union…is turning its back on us?

If they don't support us—who will?

My case is gaining attention. The local press runs a story, naming Geisness as my attorney. And *BOOM!* Enter the Teamsters, clients of his firm.

"We halted all delivery of Seattle Jap produce after Pearl Harbor, and we'll immediately withdraw our business if Geisness *defends* that Jap."

So Geisness was out. And Vanderveer. And so was the ACLU.

Art blows his stack. "Good God, what's *happening?* These Ivy League *clowns* running our country, from *Harvard and Yale,* for God's sake, are turning our Constitution into a *joke,* and no one's got the balls to *stop* 'em? Call the Seattle Bar Association, the Washington Bar, the American Bar. *Someone's* got to help us."

The result? Three clicks of the phone.

So now my defense is all up to Mary and her scrappy citizens' group. And despite the threats raining down on their heads, they dig in for the battle. And after countless letters and calls—the Gordon Hirabayashi Legal Defense Fund is born.

Art tallies up the checks. "Charles Nelson, $5. Mrs. Albert Clausen, $15. Mrs. June Riordan, $7.50, goddamn it I'm getting choked up."

I get a little choked up myself.

Lights change. Gordon writes letters.

"Dear Ellie:

"I haven't been able to eat much—haven't been very hungry. Fellows here say, 'You'll be eating like a hog by the end of the week.' I hope so. I feel so terribly ashamed of myself that I can't eat what others are eating.

"Now, Ellie, don't you go baking a cake! You know that's just what I want."

Another letter.

"Dear Woody:

"I've met my new lawyer, Frank Walters. Older, fifty-ish, Republican, American Legion member. Not someone you'd think would bat for my team, but a constitutional specialist who's game to take me on."

Another letter

"Yoo-hoo Howie!

"Here I am at the County City Building. My apartment's called "The Federal Tank." I'm the twenty-second person to be admitted to this exclusive fellowship. A couple of Negroes, swell fellas, three Japanese, an Italian, and more.

"Unfortunately, my roomie's turned out to be a Jehovah's Witness! So I'm burying myself in the books you sent: Richard Wright's *Native Son;* Oscar Wilde's *De Profundis;* the poems of Lin Yutang.

"You've got a great summer ahead of you. If you don't use it to the best advantage, I'll crown you good and proper."

He hears a noise and looks up.

"Esther!"

He springs out of the chair.

She stands there smiling, with a basket. I lift the lid: a banana cream pie.

It looks so good I want to cry. A welcome change from
hard-boiled eggs with cockroaches on the side.

Then she hands me some newspaper articles covering
my case. *The Seattle Times. The Post-Intelligencer.* She had
saved them all.

And not only that, but paper and pens, Quaker
pamphlets, some wool socks. And two books I've been
dying to read: a book on Clarence Darrow, and—

"Gordie. Taste the pie."

He does so.

"Oh my God. It's wonderful. No really, it's amazing.
Esther, you really shouldn't have…gone to all this
trouble, and…

*He meets her gaze for a moment, then quickly
picks up a book.*

"So. Clarence Darrow, now there's a guy who stood
up and took the heat, huh? That whole scandal he
weathered with the Scopes monkey trial?"

"Gordie? I skipped my chem lab to visit you."

Beat.

"Jeepers, Esther. You shouldn't be skipping class. I mean, don't you care about—"

"I care about *you*."

Beat.

"Well, gee, uh...thanks, Esther, I...um...I..."

"My folks saw your mother, Gordie. At Tule Lake last week."

"They saw Mom?

Beat.

"How is she?"

Lights change. Gordon, in dim light, as if seeing his family.

She tells me everything. Everything my family has gone through.

Boarding the train silently, crowding into worn seats.
A long whistle blows as the train pulls down the tracks.
Dad watches orchards...farms...fields...fade from view.
He asks, "Jim. After the war, will they let us come back home?"

The long ride down to Fresno, to the Pinedale Assembly Center. Days, weeks of waiting. Shipping out on another train with all the blinds pulled down. The heat. Stale air. Stuffiness. The smell of vomit and urine. And then, finally arriving: the camps at Tule Lake.

A barren desert. Row after row of barracks, of tarpaper and flimsy wood.

The dust everywhere. The wind, grim, relentless. The merciless heat. The lines. Lines for meals, for toilets. For typhoid shots, for lumber.

Watchtowers. Guards with guns.

Guns pointing *in*. At them.

Home.

> *Lights change. Gordon, taking a phone call from an outraged caller.*

"Gordie? Art Barnett. The West Coast delegates to the House of Representatives have introduced a bill to deprive you *Nisei* of your citizenship. Now, there's no way this could ever *pass*, it's a constitutional *rat's* nest, but I think you should know the score."

> *Beat. Another blow.*

"What's the press saying about us?"

"Most of 'em, left-wing, right-wing—hell, even Walter Lippmann, who should *know* better, goddammit— they're saying good riddance, Gord."

"Attorney General Biddle?"

Art explodes.

"Biddle? God, he's *useless!* Word is, *both* he and Stimson, the Secretary of War, had *opposed* this whole goddamn sorry mess as unconstitutional. But neither of them has the guts to take a strong stand with the President. Stimson's caved to the West Coast rabble, who want the Japanese farmers *out* so they don't have to *compete* with 'em, and Biddle's collapsed too, that spineless son-of-a—"

"Art! Has President Roosevelt said anything, *anything* in our favor?"

"Zilch. Zero. God! It's inexcusable! Granted, he's not famous for his "racial sensitivities"—all of his dependence on those Southern bigots in Congress—but why can't he say one word, just *one word* to defend you? The fact that he isn't, is making everything go to hell."

Beat.

"So the President doesn't see us as real Americans either?

Beat.

"Thanks, Art."

"Don't thank me for telling you news like that. If I were you, I'd punch me. And Gordie?"

"Yeah?"

"My kids said to tell you, you're still their favorite babysitter."

"Tell them thanks."

"You stay out of trouble. I mean, *more* trouble."

Lights change.

July. August. September. I try to stay on the beam by reading the letters pouring in. From people I've never met before, who hear about my case. There's a note and a check from a GI, fighting in Guadalcanal. "I'm fighting on this battlefield for the same things you are in prison. Keep the faith. Ernie Jones."

I get some distinguished visitors, like the Negro Quaker and civil rights leader, Bayard Rustin, who invites me to call him "Rusty." And some other visitors like…

Gordon looks up, flabbergasted.

"Dad!!"

As his father.

"You've got a new cellmate."

He looks Gordon over and nods.

"*Genki so dana.* You look pretty good."

"You look pretty good too."

It's been five months since we've seen each other. And in that time, our former lives have been forever lost.

I take a few steps forward, and put out my hand. Instead, he grips my shoulders, and *almost* hugs me, awkwardly.

Then he turns to the door. "Say hello to your mother."

Mom. How thin she's become! Her face is haggard and pale. Her eyes—

He grasps her hand.

"Mom? Mom—*Ore wa daijobu dayo*. I'm all right. And you...?"

> *Lights change. Gordon slams his fist against the wall.*

It's an insult. An outrage. The government has subpoenaed my parents to be witnesses against me at my trial. And my team's found *homes* where they can stay, since the owner can be deputized, and my parents still under custody. But the government says no dice. Instead, they throw my folks in jail, say *that* is adequate housing.

Dad tries in vain to cheer me up. "This way, we get to visit more." And he beams with pride when I tell him I've been elected mayor of the tank. "Mayor of the tank! Mayor of the tank! Wait till I tell Katsuno-san! Mayor of the tank!"

Still, I vow I will *never* forgive the government for doing that to my parents.

> *Lights change, sound of a gavel. Gordon in the Seattle courtroom.*

October 20, 1942. Seattle District Court.

The U.S. Prosecuting Attorney stands.

"Mr. Hirabayashi. I have two questions. Are you of

Japanese ancestry?"

"Yes. I am."

"Did you knowingly violate the curfew, and did you fail to report for evacuation?"

"Yes. That is correct."

Beat.

Judge Lloyd Black turns to the jury.

"Gentlemen, based on the defendant's answers, you are instructed to find him guilty, and if you will not you are violating your oath."

So that's *it*? Cut and dried? I'd never had a chance.

"Mr. Hirabayashi, your sentence will be as follows: 30 days for count one, and 30 days for count two, to be served consecutively, for a total of 60 days. Does the defendant have anything to say?"

"Yes, Your Honor.

Beat.

"I would like a longer sentence."

Beat.

"I *beg* your pardon?"

"Your Honor, I realize this is an unusual request. But I've been cooped up in jail for five months. And I've been told by my cellmates that I can serve my time outdoors—you know, in a road camp—if the term is 90 days. That you won't process the paperwork for anything less than that. I hope you understand that I'd really like to do this *outside*."

The judge cracks a smile.

"Well...okay. I guess I could accommodate that, I'm an outdoors man myself! Instead of two consecutive sentences, how about 90 days for count one, and 90 days for count two, to be served concurrently? Any objections?"

"No, Your Honor. Thank you."

Mom and Dad go back to camp, and two days later, we appeal. We know we'll probably lose there too, but so much the better. The Supreme Court is our aim now. This is a *national* issue.

Then the judge and I lock horns over my bail conditions. Lock horns for *four months*. And, by then, the judge is wracking his brain for some way to get *rid* of me.

Finally we hammer out a deal. While I'm waiting to hear the results of my appeal, I'll wait out the rest of my time outdoors, in a road camp.

That's acceptable.

> *Lights change. In the federal attorney's office. Both he and Gordon, exasperated.*

The federal attorney throws up his hands.

"Look. I'll say it *again*. The nearest road camp is in Tacoma, Washington, that's now off-limits to you Japanese, and after that, the nearest one's in Tucson, Arizona, that's sixteen hundred miles south of here, and we don't have the funds to *send* you."

(Desperately) "Well, what if I go on my *own*? What if I pay my own way?"

> *Beat.*

"Pay your own way...*to prison?*"

"I've *GOT* to do this *OUTSIDE.*"

The attorney leans back in his chair.

"Well...hey. If you pay your own way...I guess I can't object."

He gets out a pen and writes me a letter of
authorization.

"Oh golly, thanks. It's nice of you to do this."

"Well, I wouldn't do it for *anyone*. But I'd do it for you.
You have an honest face."

He asks how I'm planning to get down there.
Greyhound bus, I tell him.

"Well, you take care of yourself, you hear? Lots of
crazies out there. *(as one of the crazies)* 'Raaaaaaaaagh!'
And hey. Listen. You have a wonderful trip."

I leave his office with his letter, giddy with relief. Thank
God I won't be cooped up again, hemmed in by concrete
walls. Thank God I—

He stops in his tracks.

Good God.

Gordie, you've finally flipped.

You fight like hell to prove your innocence to the United
States government, and now you go and volunteer to pay
your own way to *prison?*

What the hell were you *thinking?*

I mean, it's against your principles. Especially when you've done nothing *wrong*.

So how are you gonna get around this one, huh? How are you gonna...get...around...

An idea.

Music: traveling music, guitar and harmonica, in the style of Woody Guthrie. Sound of trucks on the highway.

Gordon picks up his suitcase, throws his jacket over his shoulder, walks forward, looks left and right...and sticks out his thumb.

I decide to hitchhike. It's the perfect solution.

I wake up at dawn and walk out to a spot on the open highway. With a sack, a coat, and a suitcase. Toothbrush and a bar of soap. Kahlil Gibran's *The Prophet*. And an Abe Lincoln in my shoe, just in case I get jumped and fleeced and taken for everything I've got.

True, for a convicted criminal, my chosen mode of transport *is* highly irregular. I could be...*breaking the law*.

On the other hand, the federal attorney never said *how* I was supposed to travel the sixteen hundred miles south to Tucson, Arizona.

So, here I am on the open road…free to commit "espionage and sabotage" every step of the way!

I take the main highway to Spokane. Cut down to the Columbia River. When the river heads west, I head east. Through Pendleton, over to Baker, to the Snake River Valley in Idaho.

> *Gordon comes to the edge of a cliff, whistling under his breath.*

Wow. Get a load of that view.

> *He takes his shirt off and camps.*

I climb over rocks, ridges, and cliffs that plummet down to the river. I walk with my shirt off and get a heckuva sunburn. I wash and shave and sponge myself down in gas stations, bus stations. Sleep in ditches by the side of the road, in abandoned shacks and sheds, in fields of corn under starry skies. I light my candle on windless nights and read Kahlil Gibran by the light of the moon.

> *Lights change: nighttime. Sound cue: crickets. Gordon takes out a copy of* The Prophet. *He opens the book and reads:*

"It is not a garment I cast off this day, but a skin I tear

with my own hands. Yet I cannot tarry longer. For to stay is to freeze and crystallize and be bound in a mould. A voice cannot carry the tongue, and the lips that gave it wings. Alone must it seek the ether...

"and alone and without his nest shall the eagle fly toward the sun."

> *Gordon sits and looks up the sky, enjoying the peace and quiet.*

And two weeks later, I finally get to Tucson.

> *Sound cue: '40s country music. Gordon arrives hot, sweaty, tired. Sings wryly under his breath...*

"...where the skies are not cloudy all day..."

> *Sound cue: a dog barking. Gordon waves him off.*

Git along, little dogie.

> *Gordon puts his shirt on.*

Tucson, Arizona. The Federal Marshal's office.
It's hotter 'n the devil when I get there, a hundred six degrees and rising. Even the cactus out front looks parched.

The marshal is on the phone.

"Well, hell, how was I supposed to know he was a Hopi, damn son of a bitch looked just like a Jap. Yeah, stopped him, searched him, let him go. Christ, happens all the time—*(He notices Gordon, addresses him.)* Yeah."

"Hello sir. How do you do. My name is Gordon Hirabayashi. I'm here to serve a prison sentence at this fine facility."

The marshal stares at me.

"You…a Hopi?"

"No sir. I am not."

> *Beat.*

"Look here Jimbo, duty calls. Yeah. Catch ya later."

> *He hangs up the phone.*

"Now what's the name again?"

"Gordon Hirabayashi. *(Off his look, slower)* Hira—ba—yashi."

> *Beat.*

"That ain't Hopi?"

"Japanese."

"If you're a Jap, why aren't you in camp, Poston or Gila River?"

I hand him the letter from the federal attorney.

"You came alone…from Washington…at your own *request*? How the hell'd you *get* here?"

"Well, sir, I hitchhiked."

> *Beat.*

"*HITCHHIKED?*"

"Yes sir. Saw a lot of the mountain states, saw my girlfriend on the way, even stopped in Las Vegas and played a couple of slot machines."

> *Beat.*

"Son—you pullin' my leg?"

"Sir—I wish I was!"

He orders me to wait right there while he checks his files.

> *He riffles through his folders.*

"Hanover, Hart, Henckelson…Himmel…Hoskins…"

Beat.

"Well. Guess what. Nothing here. Looks like you're free to go."

"I beg your pardon?"

"Nothing on ya in the files. Guess you're a free man!"

Now it's my turn to stare.

"Look again. There must be *something*. Something. Somewhere. Someplace. Call the federal attorney, or Judge Black in Seattle. Call your superiors in Washington, D.C. I'm sure they've got some documentation of my criminal record."

Beat.

"I SAID YOU'RE A FREE MAN."

"Yes, and I'd take your word for it. I'd take your word and go. But someday you're going to find those papers, and then I'll have to interrupt my life, and come all the way back here. I've come a very long way. I would just like to get this over with."

The marshal scratches his head. Finally:

"Look here, tell you what. Care to see a flick? There's
a movie theater just down the road a ways, and she's
air-conditioned to boot. Now, you get yourself on down
there. Cool off. Relax. Get a bite to eat. By the time you
come back, I'll have this all checked out."

"Air-conditioned. Swell. So I'll be back, say, seven?"

"Seven it is. Go have some *FUN.*"

Light change. Sunset.

Well...I *finally* manage to get myself incarcerated. They
take me up to the mountains, high above the saguaro
cactus line, where I work the rock pile building a road to
Mount Lemmon. Befriend Hopi Indians who are fellow
conscientious objectors. Sweat through a steam bath in
a hut they'd built on the hillside. And sit by a fire while
one surmises his ancestors were the lost tribe of Israel,
"...which means we could be brothers," he said, "since
some of them could have 'dropped off' to Japan while
crossing the Bering Strait."

I look at him in the firelight. His eyes. His black hair.

Yes, we could be brothers.

Beat.

A letter arrives from Art, with the news we want to

hear: the Court of Appeals is referring my case straight to the Supreme Court. And Captain Ravisto had been dead wrong in telling me I was the lone resister to the curfew and exclusion orders. Two other *Nisei* fellas, Min Yasui and Fred Korematsu, have issued their own legal challenges, Min on the curfew in Portland, Fred on the exclusion order in San Francisco.

And now we're united in one thing: the determination to vindicate ourselves.

And in our desire to do so in the highest court in the land.

Lights change. Washington, DC.

May 10, 1943. The United States Supreme Court.

In the great marble palace, the red velvet curtains part. Enter Chief Justice Harlan Stone, followed by Justices Jackson, Reed. Rutledge, Roberts, Douglas. Black, Murphy, Frankfurter.

Our team's ready. I'm confident. I've got a new attorney, Harold Evans. And the ACLU's back on my team—when they heard we were going to Washington, they agreed to back us, *if* we refrained from attacking Executive Order 9066. My team huddled. Agreed. There was more than one way to skin a cat.

The proceedings begin.

My first attorney, Frank Walters, stands to state the facts
of my case. But the Court interrupts him, peppers him
with questions. Why are you questioning the military in
time of active war? *BOOM!* Frank's ten minutes are up,
and he hasn't even finished.

Next: Harold Evans. Who argues *unlawful delegation
of power*. If America had been invaded, and martial law
declared, Congress *could* grant the President power to
limit citizens' liberties. "But authority over citizens may
not be given to the military, when the area in question is
not a strictly military area."

"We repeat: the question has been raised whether
this country could wage a new war without loss of its
fundamental liberties at home. Here is one occasion
for this Court to give an unequivocal answer to
that question, and show the world that we fight for
democracy and preserve it too."

And now the government gets their shot. U.S. Solicitor
General Charles Fahy stands and argues:

Military necessity. "They all need to go. Every last one. To
keep America *safe*."

And that's what Charles Fahy must prove today to
justify the government's orders.

Sweeping his arm over a wall chart.

He starts with a tour of the Pacific battlefront, declaring the war "the most serious threat that has ever faced the United States." He stresses "the importance of West Coast defense facilities," "the dire need to protect them against 'espionage and sabotage'." He points out "the vast number of Japanese living *near* those facilities. The vast number who attended Japanese language schools, or attended school in Japan, who belonged to Japanese social clubs, who held dual citizenship granted by Japanese law. Vast numbers of Issei who had never become American citizens"—somehow forgetting to mention they were forbidden by law to do so. He insists that during wartime, "due process *must* give way to the military's 'reasonable discretion'."

"During time of war, it is not enough to say, 'I am a citizen, and I have rights.' One must also say, 'I am a citizen, and I have obligations'."

And now the Justices deliberate.

Gordon plays Justices arguing against Justice Frank Murphy.

"We are engaged in a war for survival against enemies who have placed a premium on barbarity and ruthlessness. Self-preservation comes first. The United States wages war to win."

Justice Frank Murphy, my champion, responds.

"But it does not appear that any serious effort was made to isolate the disloyal. Instead, 70,000 American citizens are deprived of their liberty because of a racial inheritance…"

The Justices bear down on Murphy.

"Japanese Americans have maintained here a racial solidarity which has tended to prevent their assimilation as an integral part of the white population…"

"This is so utterly inconsistent with our ideals…that I cannot lend my assent."

The tension escalates.

"I compare the orders with the military draft. A nation which requires the individual to give up his freedom and lay down his life…certainly can demand these lesser sacrifices from its other citizens."

"Undoubtedly we must wage war to win, and do it with all our might. But—"

Voices rising.

"You cannot wait for an invasion to see if loyalty

triumphs. A country that 'wages war to win' cannot sit in judgment on the decisions of its generals."

"*BUT*—it will avail us little to win the war on the battlefield and lose it here at home. We do not win the war, on the contrary, we lose it, if we destroy the Constitution and the best traditions of our country."

Lights change. The verdict is announced.

"June 21, 1943. Opinion of the United States Supreme Court.

"Where the conditions call for the choice of means by those on which the Constitution has placed the responsibility of war making...

"It is not for any court to sit in review of the wisdom of their action or substitute its judgment for theirs."

Gordon stands there, stricken.

I lost?...

A long, long silence.

They'd done it...they'd pulled it off...with a unanimous vote?

How...

I can't get my breath. I refuse to believe it. Surely the Constitution says what it says. The Declaration. The Bill of Rights. Surely anyone who can read can see it. Surely any simpleton can see it.

So why can't the...*Supreme Court of the United States of America...*

Entirely legal. Everything. Done by any other American...perfectly fine. Normal. But done by *us*, it proved...

Proved...?

That there was "military necessity" for throwing us all behind barbed wire?

Justice Murphy. *What happened to Justice Murphy?*

Gordon, as Murphy:

"Today is the first time, so far as I am aware, that we have sustained a substantial restriction of the personal liberty of citizens of the United States based upon the accident of race or ancestry. In this sense it bears a melancholy resemblance to the treatment accorded to members of the Jewish race in Germany...

"In my opinion this goes to the very brink of constitutional power."

Beat.

To the very...brink?

To the very brink?

It hits me square in the face. Hits me like a truck. How...strenuously I've denied—how *splendidly* I've defied—what I must have always known.

An American? Me? Gordon Kiyoshi Hirabayashi? Who'd grown up worshipping Abe Lincoln? Thomas Jefferson? Who'd memorized the Preamble, the Gettysburg Address? Who'd boasted time and time again, I am an American?

Well, to many in this country, to most of the people running it, to the Justices on the Supreme Court of the United States of America, perhaps even to President Franklin Delano Roosevelt, I am no more than...

a *JAP.*

Lights change. Voiceover: a cheerful army official over a loudspeaker.

After serving my ninety days, they release me.

HELPFUL HINTS FOR A SUCCESSFUL RELOCATION.

And, by now, they're starting to let some of us out of the camps.

YOU ARE LEAVING THE RELOCATION CENTER TO RESUME LIFE IN A NORMAL COMMUNITY.

And my family has gotten out and are working the sugar beet harvest over in Weiser, Idaho.

LIFE IN AMERICA TODAY IS NOT THE SAME AS WHEN YOU WITHDREW FROM IT A YEAR AGO.

And it's there that I hook up with them. They've all lost weight and look pretty scruffy, and I look even worse.

ALWAYS REMEMBER YOUR ULTIMATE DESIRE, A FREE AND EQUAL LIFE IN AMERICA. TO ATTAIN IT MAY REQUIRE SACRIFICES ON YOUR PART DURING THESE TRYING TIMES.

Most of our things in storage have been looted or destroyed. So we have to rebuild our lives, and we have to start from scratch. Which is pretty hard, considering the signs we now see in the stores: "No Japs Welcome Back Here."

DON'T SPEAK JAPANESE IN PUBLIC PLACES.

To make matters worse, my single 90-day sentence had served for two counts. And the Court used that as an excuse to only rule on one of them—the curfew. The exclusion order—the *real* issue—they didn't even touch it. So, by insisting on serving my time outdoors, I had inadvertently—

shot myself in the foot.

DON'T GANG UP IN LARGE GROUPS TO INCONVENIENCE AND ANTAGONIZE THE LOCAL PEOPLE.

"Then comes the 'loyalty questionnaire.' Are you willing to serve in the armed forces of the United States?...Will you swear unqualified allegiance to the United States... and forswear any form of allegiance to the Japanese Emperor?"

DON'T PATRONIZE HONKY-TONKS, NIGHT CLUBS, OR BARS. IT IS NOT GOOD FOR JAPANESE AMERICANS TO BE CONSPICUOUS.

I know that this might shock you, but I sit down and write a letter. "I'd be happy to answer this questionnaire if it's being asked of all Americans. However, it's been brought to my attention that this is only being distributed to people of Japanese ancestry, which would therefore be racially discriminatory. I'd like your clarification."

I stamp the envelope, lick it shut, and toss it into the mailbox.

THE PUBLIC IS SLOW TO RECOGNIZE YOUR STATUS AS AN AMERICAN. KEEP THIS IN MIND WHEN PREJUDICES AND DISCRIMINATION HURT YOU...TRY TO MAKE A FAVORABLE IMPRESSION ON EVERYONE YOU MEET.

Lights change. Gordon works outdoors.

One day while I'm mending the fence, Mom puts something in my hand: a black polished stone.

An artist named Tokuda-san had gotten the word in camp: his only son had fallen in the hills of Cassino, Italy, fighting with other *Nisei* in the 100th Battalion. And steeped in grief, Tokuda-san had found this stone in the sand. It was fall then in Tule Lake, when the blistering summer heat descends to a bitter autumn chill. And day after day Tokuda-san sat, smoothing the stone with his aged hands, hearing the cries of the wild geese as they soared beyond the barbed wire.

I look at the stone in my hand. It shines like a small black moon.

On its surface, Tokuda-san has painstakingly carved some kanji. A few tiny characters, expertly etched on the surface…

Kogen no
Ishi ni kizami
Uta mo nashi

       Gordon interprets.

I carve on this stone
from the high plateau
but I have no song

       Lights change. Twilight.

So many lost so much.

So many lives shattered. So many hopes destroyed.

My Hopi friend tells me, "You're talking out of your fucking hatch. The Constitution wasn't written for *you*, my friend, and it wasn't written for *me*." And of course I understand. What could the Constitution mean to him? A Hopi on a reservation? Whose people have known little more than American betrayal, slaughter, theft, and a string of shattered promises?

But I cannot…I *will not*…give up on the Constitution. I cannot forsake the fundamental principles upon which

I've always based being an American.

Instead I slowly begin to revise my thinking under the new circumstances.

Until now I had regarded the Supreme Court as a group above ordinary weaknesses. In my emerging understanding they become a group of mere...*people*, endowed with all the noble and ignoble qualities of other human beings.

Most importantly, I begin to distinguish between the Constitution...

and the people entrusted to uphold it.

Lights change: slowly turning to sunrise.

My failure in challenging the curfew and exclusion orders is shared by my fellow protesters. Min Yasui loses his case on the curfew. And Fred Korematsu loses his on the exclusion order as well.

The Court declares our mass incarceration is, indeed, constitutional.

But this time...it is *not* unanimous.

"Guilt is personal and not inheritable..." Justice Robert Jackson, dissenting.

"A clear violation of constitutional rights..." Justice Owen Roberts, dissenting.

"An erroneous assumption of racial guilt... The ugly abyss of racism..."

Justice Frank Murphy, dissenting.

It's way too little, and way too late. But it is something.

Something like the faintest glimmer of light.

> *Lights change. Morning. Music: a lilting guitar and fiddle.*

On my wedding day, I get up and I look around me.

Clouds are relaxing long and smooth in an Easter blue sky. Clouds resting on the mountaintops, looking like fields of snow.

It doesn't even matter that there's a warrant out for my arrest. Thanks to my rejection of the loyalty questionnaire. Yes, soon the Feds will be coming around to cart me off to prison again, so Esther and I deem it's best to tie the knot at once.

It's a simple Quaker wedding. No luxuries, no frills. We couldn't have afforded them, and of course, as a Quaker, I am philosophically opposed to them.

But Esther is radiant in a white dress, a tiny star on her hand. Yes, she has a ring.

It almost hadn't happened.

A passionate exchange. Gordon, exasperated.

"Quakers don't believe in trinkets, Ma! We don't *need* a ring!"

"*Every* girl dreams of wearing a ring on her wedding day. *Kanojo ga Kwehkah de attemo yubiwa wa katte agenasai!*"

"But—"

"I don't care if she *IS* a Quaker—you get that girl a *RING!*"

For once, I didn't argue.

When we pronounce ourselves man and wife, I hear birds trilling. As if celebrating the mere state of being free. The newspaper does a story on us: "Quaker Girl's Parents Okay Marriage to Jap-American."

But no one can ruin this day for me.

Today, there is only light.

Lights change. A sense of time passing.

When I leave the McNeil Federal Penitentiary after
serving a year's sentence for my "lack of loyalty," I have a
surprise waiting: my wife, holding a basket.

Gordon lifts the lid.

And in it: twin baby girls.

I look inside the basket. The babies are asleep. There
they are, two tiny beings, perfect, pure, complete. And,
as yet, unburdened by what a troubled world might call
them.

*Gordon slowly begins to put on his jacket and
bowtie, exchanging his 1940s glasses for his pre-
vious ones, gradually assuming the stance and
voice of his older self.*

We name our babies Sharon Mitsu and Marion Setsu.
And eventually I return to college and earn my doctorate
in sociology. And I take a job overseas, teaching in
Lebanon and Egypt. And we have another child, this
time a baby boy named Jay, and when we return home
years later, I accept a teaching post in Edmonton,
Alberta, Canada.

And the years pass, and I teach class, and my kids grow
up, and my hair grays, and one night, after a poker
game, I get a phone call out of the blue —

(Into phone) Hello? Hello? Yes, this is he…Dr. Peter, who?

A professor of political science from the University of California. Dr. Peter Irons. Who says he's just unearthed a box of secret classified documents, showing the government had suppressed, altered and destroyed crucial evidence during my Supreme Court case.

Gordon freezes. Beat.

What…?

A *Nisei* woman, Aiko Yoshinaga, had found the "smoking gun," lying on a desk in the Federal Archives. A secret report from the War Department by General John DeWitt, revealing there was no "military necessity" for our mass incarceration.

Into phone.

You're kidding.

Saying the Army *had* sufficient time to determine the loyal from the disloyal, but that the racial characteristics of the Japanese would make it near impossible "…to separate the sheep from the goats."

Go on.

And there's more evidence, he says. Documents from
the FBI, from the Office of Naval Intelligence. Boxes
of letters, memos, reports all pointing to the same
conclusion: Our mass incarceration had been caused by
racism and hysteria. And the War Department, fully
aware of this, had deliberately deceived the Court.

And he said, I'm calling to ask permission to re-open
your case.

*Several long beats. Gordon stands still, compre-
hending the magnitude of the news.*

And I tell him: I've been waiting for your call for forty
years. Let's go.

Light change. Gordon takes the stand.

And I head back into the Seattle courtroom, the very
same one where I'd been tried four decades ago. And
for an instant, in my mind, I see the faces of some of the
men who had sealed our fate: Attorney General Biddle.
Secretary of War Stimson. The President himself. The
War Department's John McCloy, who'd once declared
"...the Constitution is just a scrap of paper."

They give way now to Japanese faces without barbed
wire in front of them, faces of family and Seattle friends.
Of so many former internees, of the young Sansei
lawyers on my team volunteering years of their time.

97

A gallery of American faces…

looking up at mine.

And once again, I say it: ancestry is not a crime.

Beat.

And now in 1987, after a five-year battle, we hear a
verdict again:

**The judgments as to the exclusion and curfew
convictions are reversed…with instructions to grant
Hirabayashi's petition to vacate both convictions.**

And the room explodes into cheers.

> *Gordon takes it all in. The cheers, the historic mo-*
> *ment.*

Then press conferences. Headlines. Stories on the
evening news. CBS's Ed Bradley interviewing me for a
story on *60 Minutes*. Everyone asking, Dr. Hirabayashi,
tell us how it *feels.*

> *Several beats. Gordon, softly:*

Well.

It's been a long road to get to this point. A long and

difficult road. And even though we've come this far, we've farther still to go. But on this day...

today...

it feels like I've finally come home.

Beat. Music: an American folk tune.

My America, the one I see, is covered with squares of darkness and light. My America, the one I know, searches for self-evident truth, and sees in shreds and fragments. My America, the one I love, is not just matter, but spirit. It is before, beneath, over, above, under, around and through me.

It's a big country.

A big country.

Lights begin to fade to a soft, dreamlike state.

"*Deru kugi wa utareru.*" Dad first said it to me. "The nail that sticks out is the one that gets hit." It's an old Japanese proverb. To stay out of danger or harm's way, one should conform. One should obey. One should be inconspicuous...

unless, he told me later...

unless the hammer is smaller than the nail.

The lights narrow on Gordon.

"We hold these truths to be self-evident

that all men are created equal

that they are endowed by their Creator with certain unalienable rights..."

Beat.

I am somewhat aware of what was, and is.

I have a glimpse of what ought to be.

I seek to live as though the ought to be, is.

Lights slowly fade to black.

END OF PLAY

Made in the USA
Middletown, DE
28 February 2020